RACQUETBALL BASICS

RACQUETBALL BASICS

by Tony Boccaccio

**Illustrated by
Bill Gow**

**Photographs by
Paul Jacobs**

Created and Produced by
Arvid Knudsen

Prentice-Hall, Inc.
Englewood Cliffs, New Jersey

Dedicated to
My wife, Yolanda,
and dear children,
Bettina and Marc

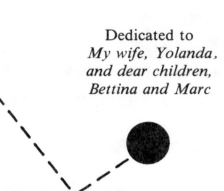

Our special thanks to the generous owners of the Royal Racquetball Club in Seldon, New York for their kind permission to photograph the players and the playing courts that you see in this book.

Prentice-Hall International, Inc., London
Prentice-Hall of Australia, Pty. Ltd., North Sydney
Prentice-Hall of Canada, Ltd., Toronto
Prentice-Hall of India Private Ltd., New Delhi
Prentice-Hall of Japan, Inc., Tokyo
Prentice-Hall of Southeast Asia Pte. Ltd., Singapore
Whitehall Books Limited, Wellington, New Zealand

1   2   3   4   5   6   7   8   9   10

Created and produced by **Arvid Knudsen.**

Library of Congress Cataloging in Publication Data

Boccaccio, Tony
  Racquetball Basics.

  Includes index.

  SUMMARY: Discusses the equipment and fundamentals of racquetball.

  1. Racquetball — Juvenile literature.
  [1. Racquetball]
    I. Knudsen, Arvid.   II. Title.

GV1017.R3B62   796.34   79-15234
ISBN 0-13-129585-3

CONTENTS

Foreword

John F. Kennedy, our 35th President, was committed to physical fitness. Early in his administration, in a major address on the subject he said, "We do not want the United States a nation of spectators. We want a nation of participants in the vigorous life. This is not a matter which can be settled, of course, from Washington. It is really a matter which starts with each individual family. It is my hope that the mothers and fathers, stretching across the United States, will be concerned to make it possible for young boys and girls to participate actively in the physical life; and that men and women who have reached the age of maturity will concern themselves with maintaining their own participation in this phase of the national vigor-national life."

He would be pleased if he could see how far the sport of racquetball has come today to embody what he had in mind.

1 THE GAME

Since racquetball is a new sport, kids always ask me how the game came about. It was started in the late 1950's by tennis players. They would practice their serve and volley on outdoor handball/paddleball courts. Even today you will see people hitting tennis balls against the wall of handball/paddleball courts. In time, people began playing ''tennisball'' on the outside courts. The same rules of handball/paddleball were used. To play ''tennisball'' players cut a few inches off the handle of their tennis racquets for better control. And so, the game of ''racquetball'' was born. Soon, players took the game indoors to local community centers, where four-wall handball was played.

The game immediately gained popularity. It was easily learned and could be played by children and adults of all ages. It was especially interesting for children since it could be played outdoors. Based on 1978 figures, there are over one thousand private court clubs and over four million players throughout the United States as compared to only twenty-five thousand players in 1970. Youngsters account for thirteen percent of the players. Private court clubs provide instructions for boys and girls including junior leagues and tournaments.

In the middle 1970's, the United States Racquetball Association was formed. The association established the rules and regulations on how the racquetball game was to be played. The association also publishes the monthly subscription magazine "National Racquetball." There are professional players in both men and women's divisions. As in tennis, pro-tours are held nationally in private court clubs.

A Little Description

An official racquetball match is played by two or four players. A match consists of three games. When played by two players, it is called "singles;" when played by four, it is called "doubles." The object of the game is to win each volley by serving or returning the ball so that the opponent is unable to keep the ball in play. A serve or volley is won when the opponent or opposing side is unable to return the ball before it hits the floor twice. Points are scored only by the serving side when it serves an "Ace" (an unreturnable serve) or wins a volley. When the serving side loses a volley, it loses the serve. Losing the serve is called a "handout." A game is won by the side first scoring 21 points or by holding your opponent scoreless while scoring 11 points. A match is won by the side first winning two games. Points are only scored on the serve.

For a practice game, I always play "cutthroat." Cutthroat is played with three players, two of whom play against the server. Then, each time the server makes an out, the players rotate and change sides. It's a lot of fun and provides a good workout.

2 THE EQUIPMENT USED

What to Wear

There is no set uniform for racquetball as there is in other sports such as baseball or basketball. The wearing apparel is similar to tennis. However, because there is so much more movement in racquetball, you will find loose fitting light colored T-shirts and gym shorts to be most comfortable. Always wear gym shoes with good tread on the soles. This will prevent you from slipping. To avoid getting blisters on your feet, use heavy sweat socks rather than light weight socks. If you're like me, you probably tend to perspire a great deal during exercise. I found the use of head and wrist sweatbands to be helpful. For my racquet hand I use a racquetball glove. To protect your eyes, I recommend using eye guards. You will find them to be quite comfortable.

Racquetballs are 2¼" in diameter

The Ball

Racquetballs are identified by numbers. The most popular balls are the Seamco 558, 559, and 444. The best way to purchase balls is in vacuum packed cans. The vacuum can prevents the balls from losing their bounce. There are two balls in a can. The official ball of the United States Racquetball Association is the black Seamco 558; the official ball of the National Racquetball Club is the green Seamco 559. The 559 ball is used in professional tours and tournaments.

The Racquet

Racquets are constructed in one piece with a head and handle. According to United States Racquetball Association rules, the head can measure no more than 11 inches in length and 9 inches in width. The handle must not be more than 7 inches long. Racquets are constructed with aluminum, fiberglass, or steel frames with wooden handles, and strung with nylon strings. The wooden handles are usually wrapped in leather to prevent slipping. However, every racquet has a nylon cord band called a "thong." The "thong" is wrapped around the wrist to secure the racquet and prevent it from flying off the hand. Based on my experience, I strongly urge you never to play without the thong wrapped around your wrist. You will notice that racquets have a plastic or rubber strip around the rim of the frame. The purpose of the strip is to prevent severe player accidents and damage to the court walls. Boys and girls use the same racquets as adults, but I recommend that children use a lighter weight racquet for better control.

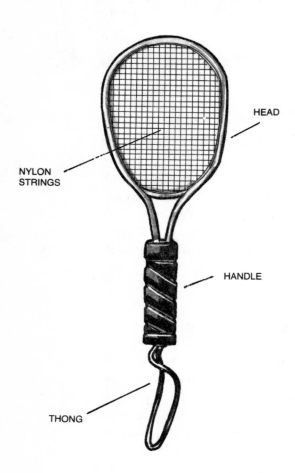

HEAD

NYLON
STRINGS

HANDLE

THONG

THE COURT **3**

Regular Closed Court

Before we learn about hitting the ball around, let us first get acquainted with the court. Racquetball is officially played indoors on 4-wall courts with ceilings. A regulation racquetball court is 40 feet long, 20 feet wide and 20 feet high. Players enter the court by a small door located at the rear or side wall. The floor is marked with either red or black lines 1½ inches wide. The ball is served from the "Service Zone." The "service line" is located 15 feet from the front wall. The "short line" is located at the center of the court; that is, 20 feet from the front and rear walls. "Service Boxes," located at each end of the service zone, are 18 inches from each side wall. Service boxes are used when playing doubles. The game of doubles is explained in Chapter 6. Five feet behind the short line "receiving lines" are marked on each side wall 3 inches from the floor.

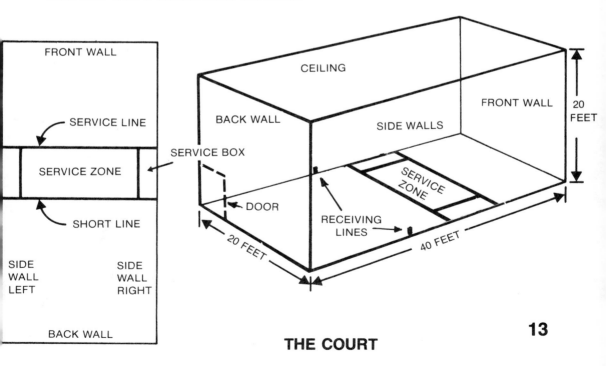

THE COURT

The Glass Court

Some clubs have an observation deck where spectators can watch the players from the top of the rear wall. In such clubs the rear wall is only 14 feet high. However, since 1976 more new clubs are using glass to construct the rear wall or one side wall with seating for spectators. The glass is about ¾ of an inch thick. Glass courts provide excellent viewing for amateur and professional tournaments.

THE GLASS COURT
VIEWING FOR SPECTATORS

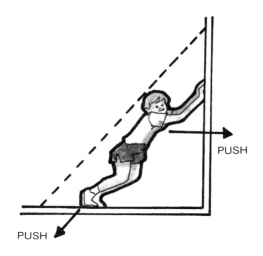

PUSH

PUSH

PLAYING BASICS **4**

Limbering Up

Let us take a moment to cover some limbering up exercises before we get into playing the game. I have found that wall stretching is the most convenient and best method for limbering up muscles before playing. Begin by facing any wall on the court. Stand about an arm's length away with your legs spread apart. Lean your entire body forward towards the wall and support yourself with your hands braced flat against the wall with arms straight out. Begin to move your legs away from the wall and adjust your hands until your body forms a triangle with the floor and wall. Then stretch your entire body by pushing with your arms and legs against the wall and floor. Stretch by counting up to 12 . . . rest, then stretch again until the count of 12. Repeat until you have had enough.

The other stretch exercise is the same as the first. The only difference is that you arch your body by pushing up and down. Again, count to 12 . . . rest, and repeat until you had enough. Then, begin to hit the ball around the court for the purpose of getting yourself mentally ready. This is the time to mentally "fit yourself into the court" and concentrate completely on game strategy, especially if you know your opponent's strength and weakness. Now you are ready to "get-em" tiger.

Playing Pointers

The game of racquetball needs super concentration. You must learn to:

- A) *Never move your eyes away from the ball or your opponent.*
- B) *Anticipate your opponent's movements.*
- C) *On a return shot develop your reflex control to hit the ball where you want.*

The player who can hit the ball where he wants it most of the time scores more points. Good reflex action is most important. But reflex must not be confused with reaction. A player with good reflex can act quickly but with control. Reflex control and concentration are the key elements of the game. A player who returns the ball with pure reaction does not have control and will lose matches. All of these skills can be developed by practicing them when playing opponents of equal skill and tested for application by playing opponents of advanced ability. The other key elements are more mechanical and are necessary for game control. Basically, there are three that you must develop:

1. *A dependable serve*
2. *Strong backhand*
3. *Play the ball off the rear wall from both sides with equal ability.*

My experience tells me that every beginner must first understand the playing basics before attempting to master these mental and mechanical skills.

Selecting the Racquet

The best way to select a racquet is by playing with it. Playing with a racquet gives you the opportunity to test the design and weight that are best suited to your style of play. I realize that there are many models to choose from and that you cannot purchase them all. But, there are two ways to make a proper selection:

1. Most court clubs rent different model racquets at a very low cost. Each time you attend the club, rent a different model racquet until you make your choice.
2. If a club does not have rentals or you do not play at a club, buy an inexpensive racquet. By playing with the racquet you learn about what you want in a racquet when you make your next purchase. Do not be surprised if the inexpensive models fit your needs.

The two important factors in a racquet are weight and handle size. Racquets range in weight from 250 to 285 grams. I always have children start with the lightest weight. I was personally experiencing pain in my arm because the racquet I was using was too heavy for me. I changed to a lighter weight one. Not only did the pain go away but my game actually improved.

The best way to select your handle size is by playing with different sizes. You will know that a handle is too small because the racquet twists in your hand when the ball strikes the head off center.

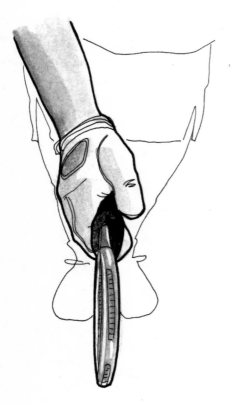

Gripping the Racquet

Gripping and using a racquetball racquet is as natural to the body as wearing a glove. With the "tong" first wrapped around the wrist, the racquet is gripped like a hand shake. When held correctly the thumb and forefinger form a "V" shape and the face of the racquet is in a vertical position. The general opinion of the more experienced players varies about rotating the racquet slightly for different strokes. However, many of us do agree that a slight rotation for the backhand stroke does help to make better contact with the ball.

Basic Strokes

There are three basic strokes in the game of racquetball:
1. Backhand
2. Forehand
3. Overhand

In the description of the three basic strokes, right-handed motions are used. Readers who are left-handed must visualize and practice opposite motions. The author is left-handed.

BACKHAND

The backhand requires more practice since the stroke is opposite your natural side. The idea of the backhand is to simulate the swinging motion and power of the forehand stroke which is a player's natural side. The main point that you should keep in mind is, "the face of the racquet must make contact with the ball in a perpendicular position to the floor and just past the right leg" (left leg for left-handed). The backhand position is with the body slightly bent from the waist facing the left side wall (right side wall for left-handed). The right arm is held at 90° and is raised, holding the 90° angle until the head of the racquet is just above the height of the player's ear. At this point, the face of the racquet should be about parallel to both side walls.

The right leg is bent slightly with feet set apart to accommodate the action of the volley. At this point the body weight is on the left leg. As the racquet is brought into swinging motion, the body weight is gradually shifted to the right leg. The left leg will naturally take a bending position.

GETTING INTO POSITION
RIGHT LEG BENT SLIGHTLY

19

During the swinging motion you must never take your eyes away from the ball. At the same time, concentrate to hold the racquet perpendicular to the floor at point of contact.

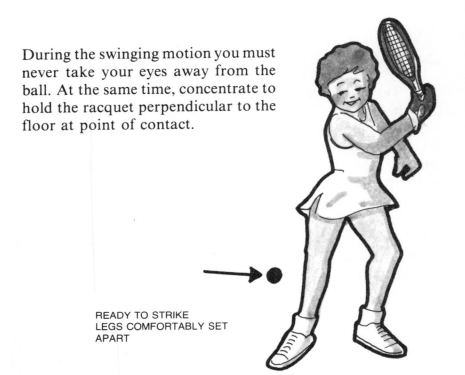

READY TO STRIKE
LEGS COMFORTABLY SET
APART

In the beginning, the holding position of the racquet will be a little cumbersome. However, with practice the entire motion will become automatic.

RACQUET

FLOOR

FOLLOW THROUGH

After contact, avoid swinging the racquet all the way around the body. The motion should stop when the arm is straight out.

21

FOREHAND

Beginners will find the motions of the forehand stroke to be more comfortable and require less time to develop control and power. Hold your racquet with the grip of a handshake and the face perpendicular to the floor. Bend your body facing the right side wall (left side wall for left-handed). The body motions are generally the same as the backhand. However, since the swing is on your natural side it is not necessary for you to think about rotating the racquet. But, as in the backhand, you must remember to hold the racquet perpendicular to the floor. Good contact with the ball occurs just past the left leg. The weight of your body is shifted the same way as in the backhand. The main point about the forehand stroke is that your arm is brought back as far as comfortable. Also, cock your wrist back, so that in the down swing the wrist is snapped at the point of contact with the ball. Keep your feet wide apart.

Remember, do not stiffen any part of your body, especially the cocking and snapping of your wrist. Your motion must be natural and loose. Also remember to bend your right shoulder and left leg so that you can lean into the ball. Leaning will get the maximum amount of force from the upper part of your body.

WHEN LEANING INTO THE BALL.
THE RACQUET PERPENDICULAR TO
THE FLOOR AT POINT OF CONTACT

—ARM BACK AND
WRIST COCKED

22

FOLLOW THROUGH.

OVERHAND—SAME MOTION AS
TOSSING A BALL.

OVERHAND

You will find that you will use the overhand stroke the least of the three strokes. Overhand motion is mostly confined to ceiling shots as an offense stroke. Occasionally a ball may take an unusually high bounce which will require an overhand return shot. Beginners use the overhand stroke more often because of their awkward movements. But, within a very short time you will develop control and your volleys will become more intense and low shooting. Gripping the racquet for the overhand is very natural because your body structure will force you to hold the racquet flat and parallel to the floor. The arm is held at about 90° and brought back by rotating the arm from the shoulder as far back as comfortable in a ready position. At this point, the face of the racquet should be facing the front wall. The overhand motion is the same as tossing a ball. This action is clearly illustrated by a baseball outfielder when he lobs the ball to the infield.

The Serve

The basic principle of racquetball is the same as other racquet sports. That is, to begin playing, the ball must be served by one player to the other. After the ball is served, the interplay between the players is called a "Volley." The objective of the game is to win each volley by serving the ball so that your opponent is unable to keep the ball in play. A serve or volley is won when opponents are unable to return the ball before it touches the floor twice. Since points can only be scored by the player or side serving the ball, it is an advantage to begin a game by winning first serve. First serve is decided by winning the toss of a coin. In all tournament events, tossing a coin to decide first serve is the official method used. In a match, the winner of first serve also serves first in the third game. However, if you win two straight games the match is over and there is no third game. When serving the ball, it is always served from any location within the boundaries of the service zone. Either foot is permitted to touch the lines, but not to extend to the outside. Extending to the outside is called a "Foot Fault." Two successive foot faults result in a handout.

To make a proper serve, you must first bounce the ball, then strike it with the face of the racquet, hit the front wall, rebound to pass the short line of the service zone and bounce before hitting the rear wall. Your opponent must stand ready to receive the ball beyond the "receiving marks" as illustrated in Chapter 3.

Losing a serve is called a "handout" and occurs when the receiver wins a volley. However, a handout can also occur from a "bad serve." A bad serve occurs by the ball hitting the floor, ceiling, or either side wall before hitting the front wall. Handouts also occur by a combination of "faults." Two successive faults result in a handout. A fault is committed when the ball hits the short line on a serve and is called a "short," or when the ball hits the rear wall on a serve before bouncing it is called a

"long." The three basic serves in racquetball are:
1. Power Serve
2. The Lob
3. The Zee

POWER SERVE

When performed correctly the ''power serve'' or drive serve is difficult for the receiver to return. A power serve which is impossible to return is called an ''Ace.'' The most popular power serve is off the side wall. From a crouching position the server brings the racquet as far back as comfortable to gain the most leverage. Then, on a low bounce, 4 to 5 inches from the floor, the ball is hit with full strength to an intended location on the front wall, such that it will rebound only a few inches high off either side wall just past the short line of the service zone.

POWER SERVE
BODY MOTIONS

ARM BACK FOR MAXIMUM POWER.

THE FOLLOW THROUGH

DOWN SWING, RACQUET HELD LEVEL AT POINT OF CONTACT WITH BALL.

Another power serve is the STRAIGHT LINE. The ball is directed to hit the front wall at a slight angle with a high velocity. Rebound, in a straight line along either side wall, several inches from both the floor and side wall, such that it will bounce only a few inches from the back wall.

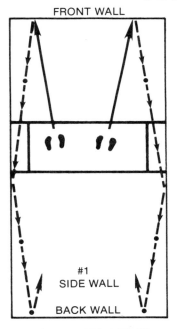

FRONT WALL

#1
SIDE WALL

BACK WALL

REBOUND FROM EITHER
SIDE WALL

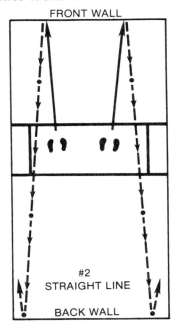

FRONT WALL

#2
STRAIGHT LINE

BACK WALL

STRAIGHT LINE, SHORT BOUNCE
OFF BACK WALL

POWER SERVE APPLICATION

All power serves have the same purpose: to score points. From the server point of view, the major drawback with a power serve is that ''shorts'' are easily committed because the ball is hit close to the floor at the front wall. And so, when a short is committed on the first serve, the server must make a *SURE SERVE* which is easily returnable by the receiver, thus placing the server in a defensive situation.

LOB SERVE

As the name implies, the ''lob'' serve is a soft hitting serve. In a slightly bent position, the server hits the ball on the bounce at about eye level to hit the top of the front wall, a foot or so from the ceiling, rebound off the front wall hug close to either side wall, and hit the floor only a foot or so from the rear wall. The closer the ball hugs the side.wall and the closer it bounces to the rear wall the more difficult it is 'for the receiver to make a return shot. You will find that the disadvantage with the lob serve is when the ball travels away from the side wall. The receiver can run up on the ball and drive it to the server's opposite side to win a handout or place the server in a poor defensive position.

LOB SERVE
BODY MOTIONS

BENT BODY

BALL CONTACT
MADE ABOUT EYE LEV

THE FOLLOW THROUGH

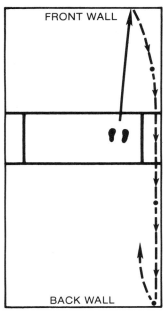

LEFT SIDE LOB SERVE
BALL HUGGING WALL

RIGHT SIDE LOB SERVE
BALL HUGGING WALL

**LOB SERVE
APPLICATION**

ZEE SERVE

I consider the zee as the more advanced serve. There are two basic variations:

1. Two corner zee   2. Off the back wall zee

Using the overhand stroke, the ball is hit after bouncing about a foot or so above the server's head.

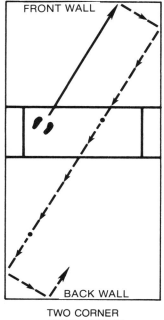

TWO CORNER
CROSS COURT

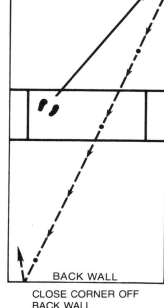

CLOSE CORNER OFF
BACK WALL

**Z SERVE
APPLICATION**

29

Returning the Serve

The serve return is important to both the server and receiver because the result of the volley will determine if the server scores a point or that the receiver wins the serve. The server has two advantages:

1. He can score points.
2. He can move immediately to the center court after the serve.

The center court position is important because you can quickly move in four possible directions: Forward, Back, and to the Left or Right side. Therefore, the idea of the return serve is to gain control of the center court position. You can do this by pulling the server away with either of four basic returns:

1. Ceiling Return
2. Kill Return
3. Power Return
4. Side to Front Wall Return

Ceiling Return: The ceiling serve return is perhaps the best return for moving the server from control of the center court position. There are two serve conditions where you can use the ceiling serve return:

1. A bad lob serve where the ball bounces a foot or more away from the side wall and to your natural side. On the return you make the ball hit the ceiling about 2 feet from the front wall and to the *server's opposite side*. The ball must be hit hard to prevent the server from setting up his return shot.
2. When a ball rebounds slowly off the rear wall. The ball is easy to undercut from the receiver's power side. Undercutting the ball causes good back spin and is difficult to return with any measure of control.

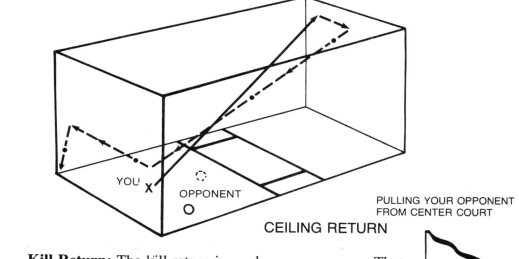

YOU X

○ ○
OPPONENT

O

PULLING YOUR OPPONENT
FROM CENTER COURT

CEILING RETURN

Kill Return: The kill return is used on a poor serve. That is, the ball speed and court location are where the receiver can coordinate his sense of timing and body movements to make the ball hit the front wall at such a low height from the floor that it is impossible for the server to make a return shot.

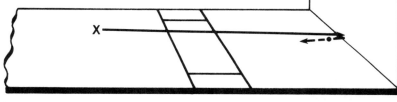

X

KILL RETURN

BALL HIT FAST, LOW
AT CROUCH OF
FRONT WALL AND
FLOOR.

Power Return: The power return is used when the serve is to your strong side. You make a return shot by hitting the ball at top speed to the weak side or to an out-of-reach location of the server. On the power return you make the ball hit the front wall about a foot or so from the floor and very close to either side wall. The ball will rebound straight back at top speed, "hugging" the side wall. Another power return is to make the ball hit the center of the front wall so that the rebound will come "straight up" on the server. The shot is very difficult to handle. This "straight up" return shot is the same as a baseball pitcher "jamming" a batter. Jamming a batter means that the ball is pitched close to the batter's hands at top speed making it difficult to hit.

31

Side To Front Wall Return: The side to front wall serve return requires good ball control. A serve that is hit at slow speed to your natural side is the best opportunity for ball control. You hit the ball at semi-speed striking either side wall (depending on the receiver's best control side) about 2 to 3 feet from the front wall. The ball will rebound, hit the front wall and bounce only a few feet from it. The speed of the ball and hitting angle will determine the effectiveness of your return. The ball must fall at least 6 or more feet from the service line. This will pull the server from the center court position. Like the ceiling return, the side to front wall serve return is the most effective shot for pulling the server away from the center court position.

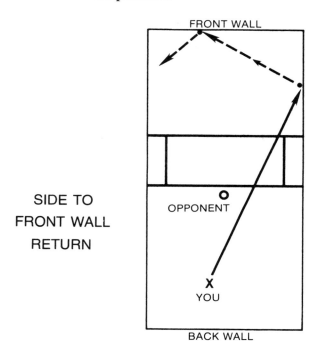

FRONT WALL

SIDE TO
FRONT WALL
RETURN

O
OPPONENT

X
YOU

BACK WALL

Playing the Back Wall

Since the ball is not permitted to bounce after hitting the back wall it must be hit as it rebounds off the back wall. This is why racquetball is referred to as a "back wall game." The only time a ball is permitted to bounce is during a volley when it travels across the court without taking a bounce. This is uncommon, but, it happens occasionally. Therefore, every beginner must learn to hit the ball as it rebounds off the back wall with both forehand and backhand strokes. Playing the back wall will require your best power of concentration. This is so because you must mentally coordinate several things at the same time:

a) Anticipate that the ball is going to hit the back wall.

b) Where it will hit.

c) The best position you must take to receive the ball.

d) Keep your eye trained on the ball while you sense your opponent's court position.

e) Know where you will direct your hit to make it difficult for your opponent's return shot.

SPOTTING THE BALL HIT THE WALL AND GETTING INTO RECEIVING POSITION

IN RECEIVING POSITION AND SENSING WHERE TO DIRECT BALL

Always stay calm, never run up on the ball and rush to hit it. You must learn to take command. You wait . . . then, at the right moment, when you feel that you have yourself mentally coordinated, you make your move. There are two things which will help you with back wall hitting:

1. You must bend to a point where you mentally believe that you have bent enough, then bend more.

2. Imagine that you have a basket in your hand and that you want to capture the ball in the basket.

FULL BENDING POSITION BALL
CONTACT JUST PAST LEFT LEG

THE FOLLOW THROUGH

Both of these suggestions will prevent you from hitting "skip balls" which is very common with backwall shots. A skip ball is a return shot that just skims the floor before hitting the front or side wall.

Finally, I have always found it helpful not to aim a return shot. When a baseball pitcher begins to aim the ball, he loses his control. Control is getting the ball where you want it because your sensing is properly co-ordinated with the motion of your body. There is a saying, "it's like threading a needle." Perhaps tailors make good racquetball players?

There is another method of playing the back wall. At times it may be difficult to make a return shot off the back wall because the player had to move quickly from a long distance to the rear court. As the ball rebounds off the back wall you are permitted to hit the ball directly back at the back wall. This kind of return is always defensive and must be avoided.

5 OFFENSE AND DEFENSE STRATEGY

Now that you have a good grasp of the basics, let's discuss some offense and defense strategy. Good offense and defense is necessary to develop the complete game. I cannot stress the importance of practice. This is especially so for children because you have the opportunity to learn and practice at an early age which will prepare you for eventual tournament competition and perhaps entering the professional ranks. For example, one of today's top professional players, Marty Hogan, started to play racquetball when he was eleven. At the age of eighteen he was the leading racquetball player in the United States. His offense shot is reported to have a speed of over 100 miles per hour.

In this chapter only names and illustrations are used to describe offense and defense shots. Refer back to Chapter 4 for applications.

OFFENSE

As the name implies, offense is an aggressive strategy. Racquetball requires an aggressive attitude. But, controlled aggression is the key to good offense and defense strategy. This means that a quality player can control his emotions to make a move only when the opportunity presents itself. Based on my experience, the best opportunity for an effective offense is the kill shot. This is so because a well-executed kill shot ends the volley. Depending on the side who made the kill, a point is scored or a handout occurs.

The best players are not always successful with a kill shot because the kill shot is a low hit ball and has the tendency to strike the floor (skip shot) before hitting the front wall or either side wall. However, to become a winner, you must develop the ability to make a kill shot at the moment of opportunity and from any position on the court. There are many variations to the kill shot. However, only the basic shots are described since others are an extension of the basics and you will be introduced to them from your playing experience.

Side Wall to Front Wall Kill (Speed Shot)

The best opportunity for making this two-wall kill shot is when you are near either side wall and your opponent is near you.

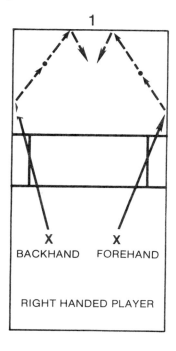

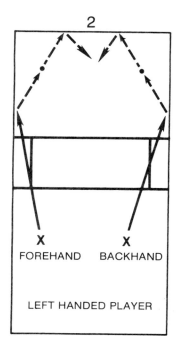

SIDE TO
FRONT
WALL KILL
APPLICATION

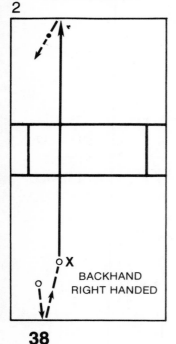

BACKWALL KILL APPLICATION

1 FOREHAND LEFT HANDED

2 BACKHAND RIGHT HANDED

Off the Back Wall Kill (Speed Shot)

The best opportunity for making the back wall kill shot is when you are near the back wall and have ample time to setup for a forehand and backhand position. Your opponent must be in back court with you. Avoid this shot if the opponent is in front court.

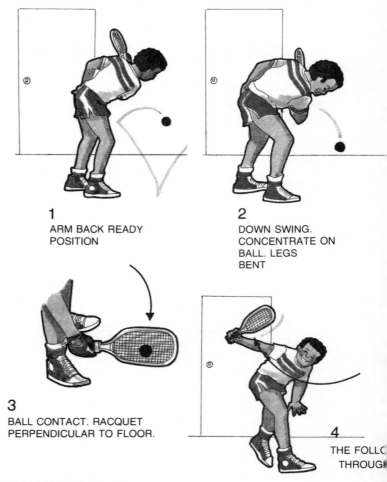

1 ARM BACK READY POSITION

2 DOWN SWING. CONCENTRATE ON BALL. LEGS BENT

3 BALL CONTACT. RACQUET PERPENDICULAR TO FLOOR.

4 THE FOLLO THROUGI

BODY MOTIONS FOR THE BACKWALL KILL
USING YOUR BACKHAND

1
RECEIVING POSITION

2
BODY BENT DOWNSWING
FOR CONTACT

3
BALL CONTACT AT
FULL POWER

4
THE FOLLOW THROUGH

BODY MOTIONS FOR THE BACKWALL KILL
USING YOUR FOREHAND

39

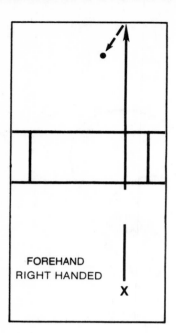

Straight Kill (Speed Shot)

The best opportunity for making a straight kill shot is when it is to your forehand side and is the most common kill since it only hits the front wall. Your opponent should be in the back court near you. Avoid this shot if the opponent is in the front court.

Drop Kill (Slow Hitting)

The best opportunity for making an effective drop kill is when you are in front court and your opponent is behind you. The ball is hit at slow speed in such a way that it drops at front court.

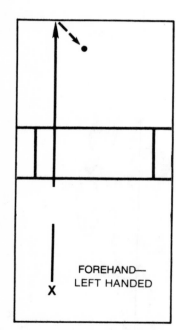

STRAIGHT KILL APPLICATION

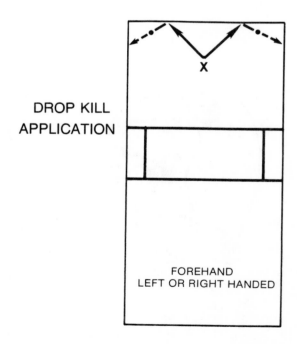

DEFENSE

Defense is a strategy to either hold or regain the offense and must be practiced as such. In racquetball, the main purpose of the offense shot is to keep your opponent from scoring points. The offense shot helps you accomplish this by slowing the pace of the volley or slowing the aggressive tempo of your opponent. The two basic defense shots are the "ZEE" and "CEILING SHOTS." For further application, refer back to Chapter 4.

Zee Shot

The best opportunity for making this control shot is when the ball is your forehand. Your position should be away from the center court and more than half way in back court with your opponents in front court at least a foot or so before the service line.

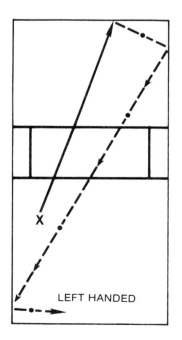

LEFT HANDED

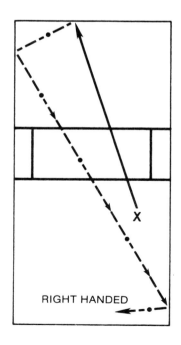

RIGHT HANDED

FOREHAND
Z SHOT

Ceiling Shot

The ceiling shot can be made from most positions on the court with either a forehand or backhand stroke. The ball is not hit hard. Backspinning the ball is the most effective means of striking the ball.

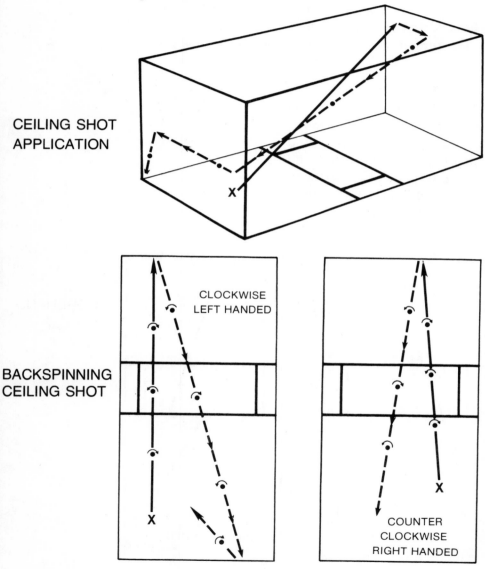

CEILING SHOT
APPLICATION

BACKSPINNING
CEILING SHOT

CLOCKWISE
LEFT HANDED

COUNTER
CLOCKWISE
RIGHT HANDED

DOUBLES 6

All of the playing basics discussed in this chapter apply to both singles and doubles. For clarity, attention was focused on the individual player. However, the only basic differences in the game of doubles are the serve and game strategies.

The Game

As in singles, first serve is decided by winning the toss of a coin. The decision as to which partner serves first is decided between them. The partner who serves first cannot alternate his turn. In tournament play a side who decides to alternate must inform the judges or their opposing teams. In a regular game, failure to do so results in a handout.

When serving the ball, the other partner must take a position in either service box with his back to the wall. The partner cannot move from the service box until the served ball passes the short line. The opposing side must remain behind the receiving lines to make their serve return. Both partners take a turn to serve the ball. Each partner is permitted 2 faults or 1 out serve. A handout occurs after the second partner's serve. However, at the beginning of the game, the side who wins first serve is only permitted a one-partner serve and loses the serve after the first serving partner commits an out serve or 2 successive faults.

Game Strategy

A team consisting of right-handed and left-handed partners is considered strong because they can each play from their natural side. However, the best success in doubles are with partners who can co-ordinate their court movements with the same ease as a game of singles. Game strategy is best accomplished with practice. The rule to remember is that only one partner takes the lead. That is, the lead partner calls the positions and location of the ball during the volley. Also of importance is that one partner plays the front court and the other plays the back court. The front court partner should be good at kill shots while the back court partner has a strong backhand and can play off the back wall shots efficiently. Calling the positions is the same as in baseball. When a pop-up is to the infield the pitcher usually takes command to call which infielder is in the best position to field the ball. When this fails, errors are committed and games are lost. Taking command of the center court position is also important in doubles. And the ceiling and side-to front wall shots are good for pulling opponents away from the center court. In doubles, however, the center position must be held at both the front and back courts.

POSTING MATCH RESULTS

Match results are posted upon draw sheets. Tournaments are broken down to the following number of players:

8, 16, 64, 128, 256

Since a match consists of three games, the results are posted after each player's name. For example, if a match went to three games the results would be posted as:

SURESHOT ARVID 21-16-21

KILLSHOT TONY 17-21-18

In one example, Sureshot won the match since he won the first and last game   21 to 17 and 21 to 18. If either player won the first two games, there would not be a third game.

A tournament draw sheet is illustrated as follows:

CHARLIE BROWN RACQUETBALL TOURNAMENT

Afterword

Now that you have completed reading about the basics of racquetball you are a real pro! Well, not exactly. You may understand how the game is played from a book but like in all things, we can only learn by doing. Based on my experience, kids who improve their game consistently play racquetball at least two sessions per week. You will find that playing against kids who are better than you will help you develop your game skills more rapidly.

Practice each day in the outdoors on your local handball court. There you can practice your serves, kill shots and backhand. If you seriously apply yourself it will not take long to become genuinely proficient in the game.

Get your Mom and Dad involved. You will find that racquetball is a great family game to be enjoyed by each and every member. Family tournaments can be great fun and are easily organized.

The values and benefits of playing racquetball are many. You will develop mental skills, muscle tone, and body coordination. In many ways it is the perfect physical exercise which sharpens up your mental alertness as well.

Playing to win is what most games are about, but good sportsmanship and manners on the court and enjoying the game are more important. But most important, have fun!

INDEX